A Man's Guide to Being a Woman's Best Friend

A Man's Guide to Being a Woman's Best Friend

by Michael Levin

Andrews and McMeel
A Universal Press Syndicate Company
Kansas City

Library of Congress Catalog Card Number: 96-85618
ISBN: 0-8362-2581-3

Design and composition by Steven Brooker of Just Your *Type*.

*This book is
dedicated to
my best friend
Susan Grant*

For all men
who want to
learn how to be a
woman's best friend

Be totally honest
about everything
even the smallest
detail

Listen to her
without interrupting

———◆———

Cuddle with her in
the morning and
bring her coffee

—◆—

Tell her to be safe
as you kiss her
good-bye in the
morning

Shower and shave
before getting into
bed at night and
then don't bother
her

Go grocery
shopping with her
on Friday night
and help put the
groceries away

Never say anything
which will cause her
to feel unworthy

———◆———

Never say anything
that will embarrass
her

———◆———

Never go into her
purse for anything

Don't dominate
conversation about
your work

———————

Give up anger you

have at yourself

———◆———

Never open her mail

Always do your best
at your job

———◆———

Establish and live

within your budget

———◆———

Never do
anything which is
embarrassing

Give her space
when she needs it

———◆———

Always make eye
contact when she is
speaking to you or
you to her

Take out the

garbage

Take her out when
she hasn't had time
to prepare dinner

Never expect
anything in return

Sometimes hold her
face in your hands
when you kiss her
mouth gently

———◆———

Prepare the
children's school
lunches

———◆———

Give her your jacket
when she feels cold

Empty the

dishwasher

Bring her breakfast
in bed once in a
while

◆

Never patronize her

Help her clean the
house

Have her car
washed and filled
with gas over the
weekend

Say thank you when

she prepares dinner

If she's employed
let her know that
you appreciate that
she's really carrying
two full-time jobs

◆

Clean the bathroom sink and wipe the water spots off of the mirror

Make love to her

Don't rush her
before the two of
you are leaving to
go someplace

—◆—

Pick your clothes
up off of the floor

———◆———

Be consistent in
your behavior and
temperament

Know when her
menstrual cycle
begins and don't
expect to be patted
on the back just
because you know

Don't ever criticize

her

Encourage her to
fantasize

———◆———

Don't smoke or abuse alcohol and drugs

Never let her see
you looking at
another woman

Be her playmate

Maintain a life
insurance policy on
yourself

—◆—

Help her examine
her breasts and
encourage her to
get a mammogram
every year

Shower and shave
before you make
love to her

———◆———

Enjoy and
appreciate the
little girl in her

———◆——

Bring her water and
something for her
headache

—◆—

Keep every promise

Encourage her to
go to her class
reunion (perhaps
even alone)

———◆———

Never make a left-hand turn with her in the passenger seat unless you are absolutely certain there's no risk from oncoming traffic

—◆—

Scratch her back in
the morning

——◆——

Be patient with

your children

———◆———

Call her whenever
you're going
to be later than
she expects

———◆———

Don't bring your
work home too
often

Never compare her
to any other woman

Never criticize

clothes she's

wearing

Share the
responsibility of
driving the children

Make sure the tires
on her car are safe

Admit you've been
wrong

Never expect her to admit she's wrong

Never comment on
the existence of a
pimple

———◆———

Hug her a couple of
times each day

———◆———

Be pleased with
anything she's
prepared for dinner

◆

Let her know
you notice and
appreciate even the
smallest things she
does for you

—◆—

Anticipate her needs

Ask her if her day
was a good one and
listen attentively
even if you know
what she's going
to say

Kiss her before you
go to sleep

Never yell at her

Let her mind be
your playground

Walk beside her not

ahead of her

Encourage her to reach for her dreams

Express your own
loving feelings in a
greeting card on
her birthday or on
your anniversary

Go to bed at the same time she does at night

Prepare your will

Never hide anything
from her

Be open and
vulnerable

Let her get dressed
in privacy

Replace the empty
roll of toilet tissue

Realize it's never
important to win
an argument

—◆—

Help her to feel

secure

Never let her come
home to a sink full
of dirty dishes

Go with her to
your children's
teacher conferences

———◆———

Practice perfect
personal hygiene

Remove the dishes
from the table after
dinner

Place her pedicure
ahead of anything
you may want for
yourself

———◆———

Make all monetary
decisions with
her and keep her
informed

Work every day on
improving yourself

———◆———

If you have not
been her best friend
until now don't
blame her if you
don't feel loved